TENNIS MEN 2025

The ultimate Reference and Hands on Book for all Tennis Fans

Florian Griff

Copyright © Florian Griff 2024
ISBN: 9798342967860

TABLE OF CONTENTS

Foreword

Knowledge

Top 20 at the Start of the Season

Tournaments

List of Tournament Winners

Top 20 at the End of the Season

Quiz

Imprint

Dear Tennis Fans!

As a passionate tennis fan, I wanted to create a book that will guide you through the entire 2025 tennis season. This book is more than just a collection of tournament schedules and statistics – it's your personal companion in the fascinating world of men's tennis.

Here, you'll find everything you need to know about the ATP and the world's best players, exciting background stories, and highlights from past seasons. There's also a fun quiz to test your knowledge and plenty of space for your own notes, so you can keep track of tournament winners and your personal Top 20.

In the tournament section, you'll always find a few symbols. First, there's the flag of the country where the tournament is taking place. Below that, you'll find the surface type. The blue symbol means hard court, the green symbol means grass, and the orange symbol means clay. Additionally, the sun symbol shows whether it's an outdoor tournament, while the roof symbol indicates an indoor event.

This book is meant to bring you many enjoyable hours full of tennis excitement and thrill. I hope it inspires you, informs you, and maybe even challenges you a bit. Enjoy reading and experiencing the 2025 men's tennis season!

Yours,
Florian

KNOWLEDGE

It should be mentioned upfront that this book is exclusively dedicated to ATP men's singles tennis and does not cover the doubles competition.

History of the ATP

The Association of Tennis Professionals (ATP) is the world's leading organization in men's tennis. It was founded in 1972 by a group of tennis players who sought a collective voice and aimed to usher the sport into a new era. Today, the ATP is responsible for organizing the ATP Tour, which is the most significant tennis tour globally, bringing together the sport's biggest names. The creation of the ATP dates back to a time when tennis was transitioning from a predominantly amateur sport to a professional one. In the 1960s and early 1970s, there were growing tensions between players and organizers over tournament management and prize money. In 1972, the players decided to establish their own organization to better represent their interests. This led to the founding of the ATP by Donald Dell, Jack Kramer, and Cliff Drysdale. A turning point in ATP history came in 1990, when the organization took full control of the professional men's tennis tour calendar and launched the ATP Tour. This new structure brought clear organization and distribution of tournaments and prize money, leading to better understanding and greater transparency for both players and fans.

The ATP organizes the ATP Tour, which consists of various tournaments, including the Grand Slam tournaments (which are organized by the International Tennis Federation (ITF) but fall under the ATP umbrella), ATP Masters 1000, ATP 500, ATP 250, and the ATP Challenger Tour.

ATP Masters 1000: These tournaments, after the Grand Slams, are the most prestigious and offer the highest ranking points and prize money.

ATP 500 und ATP 250: These categories include a variety of tournaments played both nationally and internationally. They provide important opportunities for players to earn ranking points and advance their careers.

ATP Challenger Tour: This tour serves as a "stepping stone" for up-and-coming players looking to break into the higher levels of men's tennis. More details on the ATP Challenger Tour will be explained later on.

In the 2025 season, a total of 60 ATP tournaments will be held in 26 countries, with 13 indoor and 47 outdoor events, 35 on hard courts, 18 on clay, and 7 on grass. There will be 4 Grand Slam tournaments, 9 Masters, 16 ATP 500, 30 ATP 250 tournaments, and 1 ATP Finals. After the ATP Finals (around mid-November), no ATP tournaments are held for the remainder of the year.

In addition to these tournaments, there are three more events:

United Cup: The United Cup is a relatively new tennis tournament, established in 2023. It is a mixed team event where men and women compete together for their country. The tournament's creation was made possible through the collaboration of the ATP, WTA, and ITF. It takes place before the Australian Open and serves as a warm-up event. Teams from various nations compete in a combination of men's and women's singles as well as a mixed doubles match. Each tie between two nations consists of two men's singles, two women's singles, and one mixed doubles match.

Laver Cup: The Laver Cup is an international team competition in men's tennis that has been held annually since 2017. It was named in honor of Australian tennis legend Rod Laver. The competition lasts three days and takes place in different cities around the world. Two teams compete against each other: Team Europe and Team World. Each of the three days features three singles matches and one doubles match. On the first day, each match is worth one point, on the second day two points, and on the third day three points. The team that reaches 13 points first wins the Laver Cup. The Laver Cup was introduced to bring a new and exciting event to the tennis calendar, where some of the world's best players compete in a team format.

Davis Cup: The Davis Cup is the oldest and most prestigious team competition in men's tennis. It was established in 1900 and is known as the "World Championship" of men's tennis. The Davis Cup is an international tournament where national teams from around the globe compete in a league structure. Since the reform in 2019, the format has been compressed into a final round held as a tournament with group stages and knockout rounds, all played within a single week. Nations qualify for the World Group, the highest level of the competition, either through previous results or playoffs. The Davis Cup aims to crown the best tennis national teams in the world, fostering national pride and tradition within the sport. Each of these competitions has its own unique characteristics and offers different forms of team play in tennis.

The United Cup and Laver Cup focus more on mixed-gender and continental team play, while the Davis Cup upholds national pride and traditional team competition.

ATP Finals

Another highlight of the ATP Tour is the ATP Finals, an end-of-year tournament that brings together the top eight singles players and the top eight doubles teams of the season. Since its inception in 1970, this tournament has evolved into one of the most prestigious events on the tennis calendar, offering a unique competition format with group stages followed by knockout rounds.

Ranking System and Points Allocation

The ATP uses a points system to evaluate players' performances and determine their world ranking positions. Players earn points based on their performance at tournaments throughout the year. The world ranking is crucial for tournament seedings and can significantly impact a player's career. The number of points a player earns at a tournament depends on the category and the round reached. Grand Slam tournaments offer the most points, followed by ATP Masters 1000, ATP 500, ATP 250, and Challenger tournaments. The points accumulated over the past 52 weeks (simply put) are added up to determine a player's current world ranking position.

Tournament Formats Before Today`s System

Before the introduction of today's tournament structure with the categories Masters 1000, ATP 500, ATP 250, and the various Challenger and Futures tournaments, the ATP Tour used a different classification for tournaments. This classification was based on the so-called ATP Championship Series, which existed in the 1990s and dates back to the 1970s and 1980s. Here is an overview of the previous tournament classification:

Grand Prix Tennis Circuit (1970–1989): In the 1970s and 80s, the ATP Tour was organized through the Grand Prix Tennis Circuit and the World Championship Tennis (WCT) tour. Both systems ran in parallel and had different tournaments and scoring. Grand Prix tournaments were the main events of the ATP and were divided into different categories. The most important tournaments were the Grand Prix Super Series, considered the most prestigious events aside from the Grand Slams. There were also lower-tier tournaments with less prestige and point value. The WCT tournaments were part of a competing series and also included significant events, some of which were later integrated into the ATP Tour.

ATP Tour (ab 1990): In 1990, the ATP took full control of the men's tennis circuit and restructured the tournaments. The ATP Tour World Championships were the season-ending championships, where the best players of the season competed against each other. This event counted towards the ranking and was comparable to today's ATP Finals. The tournaments of the ATP Championship Series (Single Week 1990–1995) were the predecessors of the Masters 1000. They offered varying point values, depending on the category and prestige of the tournament. The ATP Super 9 (1996–1999) included the most important tournaments on the tour after the Grand Slams.

Restructuring to the Current ATP Tour (from 2000): In 2000, the ATP Tour was restructured again. The Tennis Masters Series (2000–2003) included the former Super 9 tournaments. These events now had a unified category and scoring system, similar to today's Masters 1000. The Masters Series (2004–2008) continued the format of the Tennis Masters Series before it was officially renamed Masters 1000 in 2009. The tournaments of the ATP International Series and International Series Gold (until 2008) made up the middle and lower tiers of the ATP Tour. They were later replaced by the ATP 500 and ATP 250 categories.

ATP Challenger Tour

The ATP Challenger Tour is the second-highest professional tennis tour for men, overseen by the ATP. It serves not only as a springboard for new and young players but also as an important stage for players of all ages who want to climb the rankings and gain valuable match experience. Players who do not regularly make it into the main draws of the ATP Tour or are returning after an injury often use the Challenger Tour to get back in shape and earn points. In 2023, the ATP introduced a significant reform of the Challenger Tour to increase the competitiveness and visibility of the tournaments, as well as improve financial support for the players. This reform included a restructuring into five tournament categories:

- **Challenger 50:** This category is designed for the lower ranks of the tour, mainly targeting local talents and players at the beginning of their professional careers.
- **Challenger 75:** Ideal for players who have already achieved some success at lower levels.
- **Challenger 100:** These tournaments provide another opportunity for players to earn significant ranking points.
- **Challenger 125:** Highly competitive tournaments that attract a mix of rising talents and established ATP Tour players. With higher prize money and more ranking points, they are an attractive goal for players looking to quickly rise into the higher ATP ranks.
- **Challenger 175:** This category is new (since 2023) and was introduced to facilitate the transition from the Challenger Tour to the ATP Tour. Challenger 175 tournaments offer the most ranking points and the highest prize money on the Challenger Tour and are often held during the second week of Masters 1000 tournaments, providing additional playing opportunities for those who did not progress in the Masters event.

Terms

Beyond the basic rules, there are many terms in tennis that are important for understanding the game and various situations better. Here are some of them:

- **Lucky Loser:** A player who lost in the qualifying round of a tournament but advances to the main draw because another player withdrew after the draw was made.
- **Wild Card:** An invitation given to players by tournament organizers, allowing them to play directly in the main draw without having to go through qualifying. This is often granted to young talents, local players, or well-known stars.
- **Seed:** The placement of players in the tournament bracket based on their world ranking position. Seeding ensures that the top players do not face each other in the early rounds.
- **Bye:** A free pass, usually given to the top-seeded players in the first round of a tournament, allowing them to advance directly to the second round without playing a match.

Surfaces and Match Length

Men's tennis is played on three different surfaces: hard court, clay, and grass. Matches vary in length depending on the tournament category and phase, with formats categorized as "Best of 3" or "Best of 5."

- **Best of 3 sets:** Most tournaments in men's tennis are played in a best-of-3 format, where the player who wins two sets first wins the match.
- **Best of 5 sets:** The best-of-5 format, where the player must win three sets to win the match, is less common and is only used in the main draw of Grand Slam tournaments.

Records and Curiosities

Throughout the history of the ATP, there have been numerous records and curiosities that have shaped the sport of tennis. Here are some noteworthy records and interesting facts:

ATP Records

- **Most Grand Slam Titles (Singles):** Novak Djokovic holds the record for the most Grand Slam titles in men's singles with 24 titles (as of 2024).
- **Longest Match:** The longest match in tennis history took place in 2010 in the first round of Wimbledon between John Isner and Nicolas Mahut. The match lasted 11 hours and 5 minutes and stretched over three days, with Isner eventually winning 70-68 in the fifth set.
- **Most Weeks as Number 1:** Novak Djokovic holds the record for the most weeks ranked number 1 in the ATP rankings, spending over 396 weeks at the top.
- **Oldest Player as Number 1:** Roger Federer became the oldest player to reach the number 1 ranking at the age of 36 years and 320 days in 2018.
- **Longest Winning Streak on a Surface:** Rafael Nadal holds the record for the longest winning streak on a surface, winning 81 matches in a row on clay from 2005 to 2007.
- **Most ATP Titles Overall:** Jimmy Connors holds the record for the most ATP titles with a total of 109 tournament victories in his career.
- **Longest Grand Slam Final:** The longest Grand Slam final occurred at the 2012 Australian Open, where Novak Djokovic defeated Rafael Nadal in a 5-set match that lasted 5 hours and 53 minutes.
- **Youngest Grand Slam Winner:** Michael Chang won the French Open in 1989 at the age of 17 years and 109 days, making him the youngest male Grand Slam singles champion.

The Number 1

Since the introduction of the ATP rankings in 1973, a total of 29 players have reached the number 1 spot in the world rankings (as of August 2024). Here is a list of all the players who have ever held the top position (including the number of weeks):

- Novak Djokovic – 428 weeks
- Roger Federer – 310 weeks
- Pete Sampras – 286 weeks
- Ivan Lendl – 270 weeks
- Jimmy Connors – 268 weeks
- Rafael Nadal – 209 weeks
- John McEnroe – 170 weeks
- Björn Borg – 109 weeks
- Andre Agassi – 101 weeks
- Lleyton Hewitt – 80 weeks
- Stefan Edberg – 72 weeks
- Jim Courier – 58 weeks
- Gustavo Kuerten – 43 weeks
- Andy Murray – 41 weeks
- Ilie Năstase – 40 weeks
- Carlos Alcaraz – 36 weeks
- Mats Wilander – 20 weeks
- Daniil Medvedev – 16 weeks
- Andy Roddick – 13 weeks
- Jannik Sinner – 12 weeks (as of August 2024)
- Boris Becker – 12 weeks
- Marat Safin – 9 weeks
- Juan Carlos Ferrero – 8 weeks
- John Newcombe – 8 weeks
- Thomas Muster – 6 weeks
- Yevgeny Kafelnikov – 6 weeks
- Marcelo Ríos – 6 weeks
- Carlos Moyá – 2 weeks
- Patrick Rafter – 1 week

TOP 20 - AT THE START OF THE SEASON 2025

Name of Player   **Points**

No. 1: _____

No. 2: _____

No. 3: _____

No. 4: _____

No. 5: _____

No. 6: _____

No. 7: _____

No. 8: _____

No. 9: _____

No. 10: _____

No. 11: _____

No. 12: _____

No. 13: _____

No. 14: _____

No. 15: _____

No. 16: _____

No. 17: _____

No. 18: _____

No. 19: _____

No. 20: _____

Week 1 | 30 DEC | **Brisbane**
ATP 250 | Brisbane Int. presented by Evie

The Brisbane International takes place at the Queensland Tennis Centre, just before the first Grand Slam tournament of the season, the Australian Open. In 2006, it was decided to merge the tournaments in Brisbane into a joint ATP-WTA event to provide players with more attractive preparation opportunities for the Australian Open. The inaugural Brisbane International was held in January 2009 at the newly constructed Tennyson Tennis Centre, which features a center court named after Patrick Rafter. The past winners of the singles competition include R. Sepanek (2009), A. Roddick (2010), R. Söderling (2011), A. Murray (2012 and 2013), L. Hewitt (2014), R. Federer (2015), M. Raonic (2016), G. Dimitrov (2017 and 2024, N. Kyrgios (2018), and K. Nishikori (2019).

Singles Winner:

Week 1 | 30 DEC | **Hong Kong**
ATP 250 | Bank of China Tennis Open

Organized by the Hong Kong, China Tennis Association, the tournament is held as a preparation event for the Australian Open, classified as an ATP 250 tournament. The Hong Kong Tennis Open, formerly known as the Salem Open, began in 1973 and was discontinued in 2002. After a 21-year hiatus, the tournament was resumed in January 2024, taking place at the Victoria Park Tennis Centre. Michael Chang from the USA holds the record with three titles. The men's tournament was replaced by the Thailand Open in 2003, while Hong Kong replaced the tournament in Pune in 2024. The past winners of the singles competition include M. Chang (1994, 1995, 1997), P. Sampras (1996), K. Carlsen (1998), A. Agassi (1999), N. Kiefer (2000), M. Ríos (2001), J. C. Ferrero in 2002, and A. Rublev (2024).

Singles Winner:

Week 2 | 6 JAN | **Adelaide**
ATP 250 | Adelaide International

The Adelaide International is held at the Memorial Drive Tennis Centre and serves as a preparation event for the first Grand Slam tournament of the season, the Australian Open. After the establishment of the Brisbane International in 2009, Adelaide lost its status as an ATP preparation tournament for the Australian Open. However, with a $10 million investment from the Australian government, the facility was modernized, including the addition of a roof. The Adelaide International took place in consecutive years in 2022 and 2023. Past winners include A. Rublev (2020), G. Monfils and T. Kokkinakis (2022), N. Djokovic and K. Soon-woo in 2023, and J. Lehecka in 2024.

Singles Winner:

Week 2 | 6 JAN | **Auckland**
ATP 250 | ASB Classic

The tournament is held annually at the ASB Tennis Centre in Parnell, one week before the first Grand Slam tournament of the season, the Australian Open. Auckland hosted its first international event, the "Auckland Invitation," in 1956. The tournament was a combined men's and women's event until 1981. After a 34-year separation, the WTA and ATP tournaments were merged again in 2016. The tournament has taken place 66 times, making it one of the oldest events on the tour. Rod Laver from Australia and David Ferrer from Spain have each won the tournament four times. The most recent winners include D. Ferrer (2013), J. Isner (2014), J. Vesely (2015), R. B. Agut (2016, 2018), J. Sock (2017), T. Sandgren (2019), U. Humbert (2020), R. Gasquet (2023), and A. Tabilo in 2024.

Singles Winner:

Weeks 3-4 | 12 JAN | **Melbourne**
GRAND SLAM | Australian Open

The Australian Open is an annual tennis tournament held in Melbourne, Australia, and is the first of the four Grand Slam events of the year, followed by the French Open, Wimbledon, and the US Open. The tournament begins in mid-January and lasts for two weeks, featuring various competitions, including men's and women's singles, doubles, junior championships, and wheelchair tennis.

First held in 1905 as the Australasian Championships, the tournament was renamed the Australian Open in 1969. Until 1987, matches were played on grass courts, but since 1988, the tournament has taken place at Melbourne Park on hard courts, currently using the blue GreenSet surface. Previously, the hard court surfaces included Rebound Ace (1988 to 2007) and Plexicushion (2008 to 2020). The Australian Open has evolved into one of the largest sporting events in the Southern Hemisphere, attracting over 1.1 million visitors in 2024, making it the most attended Grand Slam tournament.

The main venues, Rod Laver Arena (with a capacity of 14,820), John Cain Arena (10,300), and Margaret Court Arena (7,500), feature retractable roofs, allowing for indoor play during inclement weather or extreme heat. The tournament significantly contributes to Victoria's economy, injecting AUD 387.7 million into the regional economy in 2020. Since relocating from Kooyong to Melbourne Park in 1988 to meet increasing demands, the tournament has experienced a massive surge in attendance.

The Australian Open is known for its fast and aggressive playing style, attracting players from around the world. Despite previous challenges posed by geographical isolation and difficult travel conditions, the tournament has continually evolved and modernized since the 1980s, solidifying its status as one of the premier tennis events globally.

The total prize money for the Australian Open (ATP and WTA) was AUD 86.5 million in 2024. The winner receives 2,000 points for the ATP ranking and approximately AUD 3 million in prize money. Unlike the other three Grand Slam tournaments, which opened to professionals in 1968, the Australian tournament opened to professional players in 1969 (Open Era). Until then, amateurs were also allowed to participate.

The Australian Open is also well-known for its fun and spontaneous performances by the players. Rafael Nadal is famous for his rituals and routines on the court. During a match at the Australian Open in 2012, he experienced a change in routine and briefly forgot the order in which to arrange his bottles. This momentary lapse disrupted his concentration and elicited laughter from the crowd as he awkwardly rearranged the bottles. On the other hand, Nick Kyrgios is known for his unconventional style on the court. During a match against Karen Khachanov at the Australian Open in 2020, he made the crowd laugh by pulling an imaginary snorkel from his pocket after a particularly long rally, pretending to take a breath to signal that he needed a break.

Serbian player Novak Djokovic holds the record for the most tournament wins at the Australian Open. He has claimed the coveted winner's trophy (Norman Brookes Challenger Cup) ten times, achieving this feat three times consecutively from 2011 to 2013 and again from 2019 to 2021. He is followed by Roger Federer (SUI) with six victories, Andre Agassi (USA) with four, and Mats Wilander (SWE) with three.

The list of the last ten tournament winners includes the following: N. Djokovic (SRB/2015, 2016, 2019 to 2021, 2023), R. Federer (SUI/2017 and 2018), R. Nadal (ESP/2022), and J. Sinner (ITA/2024).

Singles Winner:

Week 5 | 27 JAN | **Montpellier**
ATP 250 | Open Sud de France-Montpellier

The Open Sud de France is an indoor tennis tournament played on hard courts. Founded in 1987, the tournament took place in Lyon until 2009, when it moved to Montpellier in 2010. It is held at the Montpellier Arena, which has a capacity of 7,500 spectators. The tournament is one of five French ATP events held annually. No tournament took place in 2011 as it was rescheduled to a January date in 2012. Gael Monfils (FRA) and Alexander Bublik (KAZ) lead the winners' tally in Montpellier, each with two tournament titles. The past winners of the singles competition over the last ten years include R. Gasquet (FRA/2015 and 2016), A. Zverev (GER/2017), L. Pouille (FRA/2018), J.-W. Tsonga (FRA/2019), G. Monfils (FRA/2020), D. Goffin (BEL/2021), A. Bublik (KAZ/2022 and 2024), and J. Sinner (ITA/2023).

Singles Winner:

Week 6 | 3 FEB | **Dallas**
ATP 500 | Dallas Open

The Dallas Open is an ATP tennis tournament played on indoor hard courts, held in Dallas, Texas. The tournament takes place at the Styslinger/Altec Tennis Complex on the campus of Southern Methodist University. It was relocated from Uniondale, New York, where it was known as the New York Open. The Dallas Open in 2022 marked the return of the ATP tournament to Dallas, as the last Dallas Open took place in 1983. Starting in 2025, this tournament will be upgraded from an ATP 250 event to an ATP 500 event and will be held at the Ford Center at The Star, which has a seating capacity of 12,000. The list of past winners is relatively short due to the tournament's brief history and includes R. Opelka (USA/2022), W. Yibing (CHN/2023), and T. Paul (USA/2024).

Singles Winner:

Week 6 | 3 FEB | **Rotterdam**
ATP 500 | ABN Amro Open

The ABN AMRO Open, also known as the Rotterdam Open, is played on indoor hard courts and is part of the ATP Tour 500 series. The first tournament took place in November 1972, with Arthur Ashe winning the inaugural title. Since 1990, it has been part of the ATP Tour. In 1984, the singles final between Ivan Lendl and Jimmy Connors was interrupted due to a bomb threat and was not resumed (Lendl was leading 6–0, 1–0). Since 2004, former Dutch tennis player Richard Krajicek has served as the tournament director.

The singles champions over the past 10 years include S. Wawrinka (SUI/2015), M. Klizan (SVK/2016), J.W. Tsonga (FRA/2017), R. Federer (SUI/2018), G. Monfils (FRA/2019 and 2020), A. Rublev (RUS/2021), and F.-A. Aliassime (CAN/2022).

Singles Winner:

Week 7 | 10 FEB | **Buenos Aires**
ATP 250 | IEB+ Argentina Open

The Argentina Open, also known as Abierto Argentino, is an annual tournament held in Buenos Aires, Argentina. It was established in 1927 as the Argentina International Championships and was a combined men's and women's event until 1987, when the women's tournament was discontinued (after a 34-year break, the women's event was reintroduced in 2021). The men's tournament is part of the ATP Tour 250 and is played on clay courts at the Buenos Aires Lawn Tennis Club in the Palermo district, with a seating capacity of 5,500. The singles champions over the last 10 years include R. Nadal (ESP/2015), D. Thiem (AUT/2016 and 2018), A. Dolgopolov (UKR/2017), M. Cecchinato (ITA/2019), C. Ruud (NOR/2020 and 2022), D. Schwartzman (ARG/2021), C. Alcaraz (ESP/2023), and F. D. Acosta (ARG/2024).

Singles Winner:

Week 7 | 10 FEB | **Delray Beach**
ATP 250 | Delray Beach Open

The Delray Beach Open takes place annually in Delray Beach, Florida. The tournament is played on hard courts and was previously known as America's Red Clay Championships, Citrix Tennis Championships, and Delray Beach International Tennis Championships. From 1993 to 1998, the event was held in Coral Springs before moving to the Delray Beach Tennis Center in 1999. So far, only Taylor Fritz and Jan-Michael Gambill (both from the USA) have won the tournament at least twice. The last ten tournament winners include I. Karlovic (CRO/2015), S. Querrey (USA/2016), J. Sock (USA/2017), F. Tiafoe (USA/2018), R. Albot (ROU/2019), R. Opelka (USA/2020), H. Hurkacz (POL/2021), C. Norrie (GBR/2022), and T. Fritz (USA/2023 and 2024).

Sinigles Winner:

Week 7 | 10 FEB | **Marseille**
ATP 250 | Open 13 Provence

The number 13 in the name "Open 13 Provence" refers to the INSEE code of the Bouches-du-Rhône department, whose capital is Marseille. The tournament is held at the Palais des Sports de Marseille, which has a seating capacity of 5,800 spectators. The event first took place in 1993 and was initiated by former tennis player and native Marseiller Jean-François Caujolle. Marc Rosset, Thomas Enqvist, and Jo-Wilfried Tsonga hold the record with three titles each. Roger Federer reached his first ATP singles final here in 2000, although he lost that match. The list of winners from the last ten years includes G. Simon (FRA/2015), N. Kyrgios (AUS/2016), J.-W. Tsonga (FRA/2017), K. Khachanov (RUS/2018), S. Tsitsipas (GRE/2018 and 2019), D. Medvedev (RUS/2021), A. Rublev (RUS/2022), H. Hurkacz (POL/2023), and H. Umbert (FRA/2024). **Singles Winner:**

Week 8 | 17 FEB | **Doha**
ATP 500 | Qatar Exxonmobil Open

The Qatar Open is a tennis tournament played on outdoor hard courts in the Gulf state of Qatar. Until 2024, it was part of the ATP Tour 250 series and has been held annually at the Khalifa International Tennis and Squash Complex in Doha since 1993. The facility includes 24 courts and has a seating capacity of 7,000 spectators. Starting in 2025, the tournament will be elevated to the ATP 500 category. Roger Federer (SUI) holds the record for the most titles in Doha, with a total of three tournament wins (2005, 2006, and 2011). The last ten tournament winners are D. Ferrer (ESP/2015), N. Djokovic (SRB/2016 and 2017), G. Monfils (FRA/2018), R. B. Agut (ESP/2019 and 2022), A. Rublev (RUS/2020), N. Basilashvili (GEO/2021), D. Medvedev (RUS/2022), and K. Khachanov (RUS/2024).

Singles Winner:

Week 8 | 17 FEB | **Rio de Janeiro**
ATP 500 | Rio Open presented by Claro

The Rio Open was previously a WTA International event. It is held on outdoor clay courts at the Jockey Club Brasileiro. This tournament is the only ATP Tour 500 event in South America and has been the sole ATP tournament in Brazil since 2020. Before the 2019 edition, there were discussions about moving the tournament from the clay courts of the Jockey Club Brasileiro to the hard courts of the Olympic Tennis Centre in order to attract more world-class players. However, this change was never implemented. The list of winners from the last ten years includes R. Nadal (ESP/2014), D. Ferrer (ESP/2015), P. Cuevas (URU/2016), D. Thiem (AUT/2017), D. Schwartzman (ARG/2018), L. Djere (SRB/2019), C. Garin (CHI/2020), C. Alcaraz (ESP/2022), C. Norrie (GBR/2023), and S. Báez (ARG/2024).

Singles Winner:

Week 9 | 24 FEB | **Acapulco**
ATP 500 | Abierto Mexicano Telcel

The Mexican Open has been held at the Arena GNP Seguros in Acapulco since 2022, after previously being hosted at the Fairmont Acapulco Princess, also in Acapulco. Until 2013, the tournament was played on red clay courts before switching to hard courts in 2014. The Mexican Open was held in Mexico City from 1993 to 1998, and again in 2000, before being relocated to Acapulco in 2001. The winner traditionally receives a large silver pumpkin trophy. Rafael Nadal and David Ferrer hold the record for the most tournament victories, with four titles each. The recent champions include D. Ferrer (ESP/2015), D. Thiem (AUT/2016), S. Querrey (USA/2017), J. M. del Potro (ARG/2018), N. Kyrgios (AUS/2019), R. Nadal (ESP/2020 and 2022), A. Zverev (GER/2021), and A. de Minaur (AUS/2023 and 2024).

Singles Winner:

Week 9 | 24 FEB | **Dubai**
ATP 500 | Dubai Duty Free Tennis Championships

This tournament held annually on outdoor hard courts in Dubai, United Arab Emirates. The event takes place at the end of February and includes both men's and women's competitions. It is held under the patronage of Sheikh Mohammed bin Rashid Al Maktoum. In 2001, the tournament was upgraded to the ATP 500 category. The event has been hosted at the newly built Dubai Tennis Stadium in the Aviation Club, which has a seating capacity of 5,000, since 1996. Roger Federer holds the local record with 8 tournament victories. The champions over the last 10 years include R. Federer (SUI/2015 and 2019), S. Wawrinka (SUI/2016), A. Murray (GBR/2017), R. B. Agut (ESP/2018), N. Djokovic (SRB/2020), A. Karatsev (RUS/2021), A. Rublev (RUS/2022), D. Medvedev (RUS/2023), and H. Humbert (FRA/2024).

Singles Winner:

Week 9 | 24 FEB | **Santiago de Chile**
ATP 250 | Movistar Chile Open

The Chilean Open has been held in Chile since 1976, with interruptions from 1984-1992 and 2015-2019. It is part of the ATP 250 series. The tournament has been hosted in Santiago (1976-1981, 1993-2000, 2010-2011, and since 2020) and Viña del Mar (1981-1983, 2001-2009, and 2012-2014). In week 9 of 2025, the tournament will be held alongside the ATP 500 events in Dubai and Acapulco. It is one of the most important tournaments in Latin America and was part of the "Golden Tour" along with the tournaments in Buenos Aires, Córdoba, and Rio de Janeiro. The courts in Santiago tend to be slippery due to the Mediterranean climate, while the courts in Viña del Mar are slower because of the high humidity. The tournament trophy features six copper, triangular leaves representing the Andes Mountains, set on a black base. Chilean player Fernando González holds the local record with four tournament titles.

The tournament winners over the last 10 years include T. Bellucci (BRA/2010), T. Robredo (ESP/2011), J. Mónaco (ARG/2012), H. Zeballos (ARG/2013), F. Fognini (ITA/2014), T. S. Wild (BRA/2020), C. Garín (CHI/2021), P. Martínez (ESP/2022), N. Jarry (CHI/2023), and S. Báez (CHI/2024).

Singles Winner:

Weeks 10-11 | 5 MAR | **Indian Wells**
ATP MASTERS 1000 | BNP Paribas Open

The Indian Wells Open takes place in March on outdoor hard courts. The tournament is part of the ATP Masters 1000 series and the WTA 1000 series. It is the most attended tennis tournament outside of the four Grand Slams and is often referred to as the "fifth Grand Slam." The Indian Wells Tennis Garden is home to the second-largest permanent tennis stadium in the world, after the Arthur Ashe Stadium in New York. The Indian Wells Open is the most important tennis event in the western United States and the second-largest in the entire U.S. and Americas after the US Open. It is the first event in the "Sunshine Double" series, followed by the Miami Open.

From 1974 to 1976, the event was non-tour, and from 1977 to 1989, it was part of the Grand Prix Tennis Tour. Indian Wells is located in the Coachella Valley, about 200 km east of Los Angeles. The Indian Wells Tennis Garden, built in 2000, has 29 courts, including the main stadium with a seating capacity of 16,100, making it the second-largest tennis-specific stadium in the world. After the 2013 BNP Paribas Open, the venue underwent expansions and upgrades, including a new 8,000-seat Stadium 2. The revamp also included a "Pro Purple" court, specifically designed for the ATP Masters Series, as the purple color contrasts sharply with the yellow tennis balls.

Roger Federer (SUI) and Novak Djokovic (SRB) are tied as the record holders for the most titles at Indian Wells, with 5 wins each. The winners over the past 10 years are N. Djokovic (SRB/2014–2016), R. Federer (SUI/2017), J. M. del Potro (ARG/2018), D. Thiem (AUT/2019), C. Norrie (GBR/2021), T. Fritz (USA/2022), and C. Alcaraz (ESP/2023 and 2024).

Singles Winner:

Weeks 12-13 | 19 MAR | **Miami**
ATP MASTERS 1000 | Miami Open p. by ITAÚ

The Miami Open takes place annually in Miami Gardens, Florida, on outdoor hard courts at the Hard Rock Stadium. It is part of the ATP Masters 1000 and WTA 1000 events. The tournament was held at the Tennis Center in Crandon Park, Key Biscayne, from 1987 to 2018, before moving to Miami Gardens in 2019. It is the second event in the "Sunshine Double" series, following the Indian Wells Open. In 2023, the tournament recorded over 386,000 attendees, making it one of the largest tennis events outside the four Grand Slams.

The Hard Rock Stadium, primarily used for American football (with a seating capacity of 14,000), offers a modified seating arrangement with temporary stands for the Center Court, while new permanent courts were constructed in the stadium's parking lots. The Miami Open is one of the few tournaments outside the Grand Slams that features a singles draw larger than 64 players, extending beyond one week. The singles competition includes 96 men and 96 women and spans 12 days.

A memorable moment occurred during the 2018 tournament when Australian player Thanasi Kokkinakis faced world No. 1 Roger Federer in the second round. A spectator humorously shouted, "Let's go, Kokkinut!" during the match, which made both the crowd and players laugh. This unique nickname seemingly boosted Kokkinakis' spirits as he went on to upset Federer in a surprising victory.

Andre Agassi (USA) and Novak Djokovic (SRB) hold the record for most Miami Open titles with six each. The champions over the past 10 years include N. Djokovic (SRB/2014-2016), R. Federer (SUI/2017 and 2019), J. Isner (USA/2018), H. Hurkacz (POL/2021), C. Alcaraz (ESP/2022), D. Medvedev (RUS/2023), and J. Sinner (ITA/2024).

Singles Winner:

Week 14 | 31 MAR | **Bucharest**
ATP 250 | Tiriac Open

The Romanian Open, also known as the BRD Năstase Țiriac Trophy, is played on outdoor clay courts. Since 1993, the tournament has been held annually in Bucharest, Romania, with a break from 2017 to 2023 when it was relocated to Budapest, Belgrade, or Banja Luka. The tournament is named in honor of the famous Romanian tennis players Ilie Năstase and Ion Țiriac. No Romanian player has won the singles title yet, although Victor Hănescu reached the final in 2007. Gilles Simon (FRA) holds the record for most titles at the event, having won it three times. The singles champions from the last 10 years include G. Simon (FRA/2008 and 2012), A. Montanes (ESP/2009), J. I. Chela (ARG/2010), F. Mayer (GER/2011), L. Rosol (CZE/2013), G. Dimitrov (BUL/2014), G. Garcia-Lopez (ESP/2015), F. Verdasco (ESP/2016), and M. Fucsovics (HUN/2024).

Singles Winner:

Week 14 | 31 MAR | **Houston**
ATP 250 | F. S. & Co US Men's Clay Court Champ.

The tournament was founded in 1910 and has taken place in nearly two dozen cities; since 2001, it has been held in Houston. It is the only remaining ATP tournament in the USA that is played on clay courts. From 2001 to 2007, the tournament was hosted at the Houston Westside Tennis Club. In 2007, the surface changed from red clay to green clay. That same year, a new venue was sought, and the River Oaks Country Club in Houston was selected, featuring a stadium with a seating capacity of 3,000.

Frank Parker and Jimmy Connors (both USA) have each won the tournament four times. The winners from the last 10 years include J. Isner (USA/2013), F. Verdasco (ESP/2014), J. Sock (USA/2015), J. Monaco (ARG/2016), S. Johnson (USA/2017 and 2018), C. Garin (CHI/2019), R. Opelka (USA/2022), F. Tiafoe (USA/2023), and B. Shelton (USA/2024).

Singles Winner:

Week 14 | 31 MAR | **Marrakech**
ATP 250 | Grand Prix Hassan II

The Grand Prix Hassan II is an annual tennis tournament that belongs to the ATP Tour 250 series. It is played on clay courts and was held until 2015 at the Complexe Al Amal in Casablanca, Morocco. Since 2016, the tournament has been hosted in Marrakech at the Royal Tennis Club de Marrakech. Between 1984 and 1989, it was part of the Challenger Series. The Grand Prix Hassan II is currently the only ATP tournament in Africa. The event usually takes place in April but has also been held in March, serving as a preparatory tournament for the French Open.

The winners list from Marrakech includes F. Delbonis (ARG/2016), B. Coric (CRO/2017), P. Andujar (ESP/2018), B. Paire (FRA/2019), D. Goffin (BEL/2022), R. Carballes Baena (ESP/2023), and M. Berrettini (ITA/2024).

Singles Winner:

Week 15 | 6 APR | **Monte-Carlo**
ATP MASTERS 1000 | Rolex Monte-Carlo Masters

The Monte-Carlo Masters takes place in Roquebrune-Cap-Martin, France, making it the only tournament on the tour not played in its actual host country. It is held on clay courts at the Monte Carlo Country Club (seating capacity: 10,000) in April and is one of the nine ATP Tour Masters 1000 events. The venue is known for its picturesque location overlooking the Mediterranean Sea, offering spectacular views and a unique atmosphere that captivates both players and spectators. The tournament was founded in 1896 as the Monte-Carlo International and is considered one of the most traditional tennis tournaments.

Originally, the tournament was played on red shale at the Lawn Tennis de Monte-Carlo beneath the Grand Hôtel de Paris until it was moved to La Condamine in 1905. It was played there from 1907 to 1914 and again in 1920. Afterward, the tournament was briefly held on the roof of a garage in Beausoleil before moving to the "La Festa Country Club" in 1921. Since 2009, the Monte Carlo Masters has been the only Masters tournament without mandatory player participation from top players.

Rafael Nadal (ESP) won the tournament eight consecutive times from 2005 to 2012 and secured his eleventh title in 2018, setting a record. Nadal is renowned for his dominance on clay courts. After one of his victories, something unexpected happened: during the award ceremony, the trophy slipped from his hands and broke. Fortunately, the trophy was later repaired.

The winners list from the last 10 years includes S. Wawrinka (SUI/2014), N. Djokovic (SRB/2015), R. Nadal (ESP/2016 to 2018), F. Fognini (ITA/2019), S. Tsitsipas (GRE/2021, 2022, and 2024), and A. Rublev (RUS/2023).

Singles Winner:

Week 16 | 14 APR | **Barcelona**
ATP 500 | Barcelona Open Banc Sabadell

The Barcelona Open was founded in 1953 and was held as a combined men's and women's tournament until 1980. It takes place at the Real Club de Tenis Barcelona on clay courts and is commonly known as the Trofeo Conde de Godó. The tournament was initiated by Carlos Godó Valls after the tennis club moved to its new location in Pedralbes.

Spanish player Rafael Nadal has won the singles title an unprecedented twelve times, which is why the center court of the Real Club de Tenis Barcelona has been renamed the Pista Rafa Nadal (Rafa Nadal Arena).

The tournament winners of the last 10 years are K. Nishikori (JPN/2014 and 2015), R. Nadal (ESP/2016-2018, 2021), D. Thiem (AUT/2019), C. Alcaraz (ESP/2022 and 2023), and C. Ruud (NOR/2024).

Singles Winner:

Week 16 | 14 APR | **Munich**
ATP 500 | BMW Open

In 1900, the Munich Tennis and Lawn Club (MTTC) Iphitos hosted the first International Tennis Championships of Bavaria on grass courts. Since 1990, the tournament has been held as an ATP Tour 250 event, and from 2025, it will be classified as an ATP 500 tournament. The winner receives not only prize money but also a car from BMW. In 2022, the Allianz Para Trophy was introduced as part of the BMW Open, which will be part of the ITF-1 Series of the UNIQLO Wheelchair Tennis Tour in 2024. The renovated facility is set to accommodate 6,000 spectators.

The list of winners from the last 10 years includes: M. Klizan (SVK/2014), A. Murray (GBR/2015), P. Kohlschreiber (GER/2016), A. Zverev (GER/2017 and 2018), C. Garin (CHI/2019), N. Basilashvili (GEO/2021), H. Rune (DEN/2022 and 2023), and J. L. Struff (GER/2024).

Singles Winner:

Weeks 17-18 | 23 APR | **Madrid**
ATP MASTERS 1000 | Mutua Madrid Open

The Madrid Open (also known as the Mutua Madrid Open) is held on clay courts at the Caja Mágica. The main stadium features a retractable roof. The tournament was established in 2002 as a men's-only event and was held as an indoor hard court tournament until 2008, before moving to outdoor clay courts in 2009.

From 2009 to 2021, the tournament was owned by Romanian businessman and former ATP player Ion Țiriac, who sold it to IMG for approximately €390 million. The tournament generates over €107 million annually for Madrid. Since 2019, Feliciano López has served as tournament director, further connecting the event to a popular active Spanish player. Starting in 2023, the tournament is held over two weeks, similar to the Masters events in Indian Wells and Miami.

A notable episode was the introduction of blue clay courts in 2012, which were eliminated the following year due to player protests regarding the surface's slipperiness.

Roger Federer is the only male player to have won the tournament on three different surfaces: hard court (2006), red clay (2009), and blue clay (2012). However, Rafael Nadal holds the record with a total of five local tournament wins, followed by Novak Djokovic (SRB) and Roger Federer (SUI) with three tournament wins each.

The winners of the last 10 years include R. Nadal (ESP/2014 and 2017), A. Murray (GBR/2015), N. Djokovic (SRB/2016 and 2019), A. Zverev (GER/2018 and 2021), C. Alcaraz (2022 and 2023), and A. Rublev (RUS/2024).

Singles Winner:

Weeks 19-20 | 7 MAY | **Rome**
ATP MASTERS 1000 | Internazionali BNL d'Italia

The Italian Open (Italian: Internazionali d'Italia) is held on clay courts at the Foro Italico. It is part of the ATP Masters 1000 events on the ATP Tour and the WTA 1000 events on the WTA Tour. The two tournaments were merged in 2011. Spain's Rafael Nadal holds the record with ten men's singles titles, followed by Novak Djokovic with six (who has also reached the finals there six additional times).

The tournament was first initiated in 1930 in Milan at the Tennis Club of Count Alberto Bonacossa and was held in Milan until 1934, before moving to Rome at the Foro Italico in 1935. In 1961, the tournament was held in Turin but later returned to Rome. Since 1990, it has been part of the ATP Championship Series Single Week tournaments, now known as ATP Tour Masters 1000. Starting in 2023, the tournament is held over two weeks, similar to the Masters 1000 events in Indian Wells and Miami.

The tournament takes place at the Foro Italico Tennis Center, which has 18 clay courts. Nine of these are used for the tournament, while the others are designated for practice. There are three main stadiums: the central stadium, Stadio Centrale, with 10,400 seats; Stadio Pietrangeli, with 3,500 seats; and the Grand Stand Arena. Players and spectators sometimes touch the foot of a specific bronze statue at the Foro Italico, believing it brings good luck. These aspects make the Italian Open one of the most significant tennis tournaments in the world.

The winners of the last 10 years include N. Djokovic (SRB/2015, 2020, and 2022), A. Murray (GBR/2016), A. Zverev (GER/2017 and 2024), R. Nadal (ESP/2018, 2019, and 2021), and D. Medvedev (RUS/2023).

Singles Winner:

Week 21 | 18 MAY | **Hamburg**
ATP 500 | Hamburg Open

The ATP tournament in Hamburg, known as the Hamburg European Open, takes place at the Rothenbaum in Hamburg. It was part of the ATP Masters Series until 2008 and was known as the Hamburg Masters. Since 2009, it has been a part of the ATP Tour 500. In addition to the men's tournament, women's events were held from 1896 to 2002, and since 2021, a parallel women's tournament has been reintroduced.

Swiss player Roger Federer holds the local record with a total of four titles. The winners of the last 10 years include L. Mayer (ARG/2014 and 2017), R. Nadal (ESP/2015), M. Klizan (SVK/2016), N. Basilashvili (GEO/2018 and 2019), A. Rublev (RUS/2020), P. Carreno Busta (ESP/2021), L. Musetti (ITA/2022), A. Zverev (GER/2023), and A. Fils (FRA/2024).

Singles Winner:

Week 21 | 18 MAY | **Geneva**
ATP 250 | Gonet Geneva Open

The Geneva Open is a tennis tournament that took place annually on clay courts in Geneva from 1980 to 1991. From 1992 to 2014, Geneva served as the venue for a Challenger tournament. In 2014, it was decided to move the tournament from Düsseldorf to Geneva and host it as an ATP 250 event starting in 2015.

Casper Ruud holds the record for singles titles with three victories, while Mate Pavić holds the doubles record with four wins—two with Oliver Marach, one with Nikola Mektić, and one with Marcelo Arévalo. Balázs Taróczy from Hungary is the only player to have won both the singles and doubles titles in the same year. The winners since 2015 include T. Bellucci (BRA/2015), S. Wawrinka (SUI/2016 and 2017), M. Fucsovics (HUN/2018), A. Zverev (GER/2019), C. Ruud (NOR/2021, 2022, and 2024), and N. Jarry (CHI/2023).

Singles Winner:

Weeks 22-23 | 25 MAY | **Paris**
GRAND SLAM | Roland-Garros

The French Open, also known as Roland-Garros, is held annually at the Stade Roland Garros in Paris. The venue features three main courts: Court Philippe Chatrier (15,265 seats), Court Suzanne Lenglen (10,068 seats), and Court Simonne Mathieu (5,000 seats). It is the only Grand Slam tournament played on clay courts and the second of the four Grand Slam events each year, following the Australian Open and preceding Wimbledon and the US Open.

The tournament has a long history dating back to 1891 when it was held as the Championnat de France exclusively for members of French clubs. In 1928, it moved to its current location, named after the World War I pilot Roland Garros, after the French Davis Cup team, known as the "Four Musketeers" (René Lacoste, Jean Borotra, Henri Cochet, and Jacques Brugnon), won the Davis Cup on American soil. The tournament did not take place during World War II, but since 1968, both amateurs and professionals have been allowed to participate. This made the French Open the first "Open" tournament among the Grand Slams. Since 2007, equal prize money has been awarded to both men and women in all rounds.

The clay surface of the French Open is unique among the Grand Slams and presents specific challenges. The clay slows down the game and causes higher ball bounces, making it difficult for players with strong serves and serve-and-volley tactics. For example, Pete Sampras, who has won 14 Grand Slam titles, never won the French Open, with his best result being a semifinal appearance in 1996. Conversely, players like Rafael Nadal, regarded as one of the greatest clay court players of all time, along with Björn Borg and Ivan Lendl, who excel on clay, have had tremendous success at Roland Garros. Rafael Nadal has won the tournament 14 times and holds numerous records.

The trophy for the men's singles champion is the Coupe des Mousquetaires, named in honor of the "Four Musketeers." This trophy weighs 14 kg and remains the property of the French Tennis Federation (FFT), while the winners receive a smaller replica.

The French Open is considered one of the most physically demanding tournaments in tennis due to the seven rounds required to win the title, the clay court conditions, and the best-of-five matches in men's singles. Players and fans appreciate the tournament not only for its challenges but also for its tradition and the unique atmosphere that the Stade Roland Garros provides.

In 2004, French players Fabrice Santoro and Arnaud Clément played the longest singles match in the history of the French Open. The match lasted 6 hours and 33 minutes over two days, concluding with a victory for Santoro. In 1989, 17-year-old Michael Chang became the youngest player to win the French Open. In a legendary quarterfinal against Ivan Lendl, then the world's top player, Chang executed an unexpected and audacious underarm serve to disrupt Lendl's rhythm, ultimately winning the match and later the tournament.

In addition to record-holder Rafael Nadal, who has the most local tournament wins, other notable players include Björn Borg (SWE) with 6 titles, Mats Wilander (SWE), Ivan Lendl (CZE), Novak Djokovic (SRB), and Gustavo Kuerten (BRA), each with 3 titles.

The following gentlemen have held the Coupe des Mousquetaires in the last 10 years: S. Wawrinka (SUI/2015), N. Djokovic (SRB/2016, 2021, and 2023), R. Nadal (ESP/2017 to 2020 and 2022), and C. Alcaraz (ESP/2024).

Singles Winner:

Week 24 | 9 JUN | 'S-Hertogenbosch
ATP 250 | Libema Open

The Rosmalen Grass Court Championships take place in Rosmalen, near 's-Hertogenbosch in the Netherlands. The tournament is held on grass courts at the Autotron Congress Center. In 1989, an invitational tournament featuring eight players was held, which was won by Miloslav Mečíř. In 1990, the tournament became part of the newly established ATP Tour and was officially named the Continental Grass Court Championships. The tournament serves as a preparation event for professional players ahead of the Wimbledon Championships. The winners of the last 10 years are as follows: N. Mahut (FRA/2013, 2015, and 2016), R. Bautista Agut (ESP/2014), G. Müller (LUX/2017), R. Gasquet (FRA/2018), A. Mannarino (FRA/2019), T. van Rijthoven (NED/2022), T. Griekspoor (NED/2023), and A. de Minaur (AUS/2024).

Singles Winner:

Week 24 | 9 JUN | **Stuttgart**
ATP 250 | Boss Open

The month of June is all about the grass season on the ATP Tour. The ATP tournament in Stuttgart is held at the TC Weissenhof tennis facility, which was opened in 1914, and the Center Court has a capacity of 6,500 spectators.

In 1990, it became a founding member of the ATP Championship Series, the predecessor to the ATP Tour 500 Series (until 2008). Since 2015, the tournament has been played on grass instead of clay, serving as a preparation event for Wimbledon, with the aim of attracting a more competitive field.

The list of winners from the last 10 years includes R. Bautista Agut (ESP/2014), R. Nadal (ESP/2015), D. Thiem (AUT/2016), L. Pouille (FRA/2017), R. Federer (SUI/2018), M. Berrettini (ITA/2019 and 2022), M. Cilic (CRO/2022), F. Tiafoe (USA/2023), and J. Draper (USA/2024).

Singles Winner:

Week 25 | 16 JUN | **Halle**
ATP 500 | Terra Wortmann Open

The ATP tournament in Halle (Westphalia) serves as an important preparation event for Wimbledon, just like other grass tournaments. The tournament was first held in 1993 and has been part of the ATP Tour 500 since 2015. The venue, the OWL Arena, features a Center Court (with a retractable roof) that has a capacity of 11,500 spectators, as well as a second court with 3,500 seats. Since 2008, a special grass aeration system has ensured optimal playing conditions. Swiss player Roger Federer is the undisputed record holder for local tournament victories, with a total of 10 titles. The winners over the last 10 years include R. Federer (SUI/2014, 2015, and 2019), F. Mayer (GER/2016), B. Coric (CRO/2018), U. Humbert (FRA/2021), H. Hurkacz (POL/2022), A. Bublik (KAZ/2023), and J. Sinner (ITA/2024).

Singles Winner:

Week 25 | 16 JUN | **London**
ATP 500 | Cinch Championships

The Queen's Club Championships are held at the Queen's Club in West Kensington. Andy Murray (GBR) holds the local record with five titles. The tournament, originally known as the London Athletic Club Tournament, was founded in 1881, making it one of the oldest tournaments in the world. In 2015, it was upgraded from an ATP 250 to an ATP 500 tournament and has been voted ATP Tournament of the Year multiple times. In 2004, Andy Roddick (USA) set the then-world record for the fastest serve at the tournament, clocking in at 153 mph (246.2 km/h).

The winners of the tournament over the last 10 years include G. Dimitrov (BUL/2014), A. Murray (GBR/2015 and 2016), F. Lopez (ESP/2017 and 2019), M. Cilic (CRO/2018), M. Berrettini (ITA/2021 and 2022), C. Alcaraz (ESP/2023), and T. Paul (USA/2024).

Singles Winner:

Week 26 | 22 JUN | **Mallorca**
ATP 250 | Mallorca Championships

The Mallorca Championships are held on the grass courts of the Mallorca Country Club in Santa Ponsa, located on the Balearic Island of Mallorca. Initially, the event was part of the WTA Tour, but since 2021, the men's ATP players have competed at the tournament, while the WTA discontinued their matches on the island in the same year.

So far, four different players have won the ATP tournament: D. Medvedev (RUS/2021), S. Tsitsipas (GRE/2022), C. Eubanks (USA/2023), and A. Tabilo (CHI/2024).

Singles Winner:

Week 26 | 23 JUN | **Eastbourne**
ATP 250 | Rothesay International

The Eastbourne International is part of both the WTA Tour and the ATP Tour. It is held at the Devonshire Park Lawn Tennis Club in Eastbourne and has been staged since 1974. Between 2009 and 2014, it replaced the Nottingham Open as a grass-court event, but when Nottingham returned from 2015 to 2016, Eastbourne did not hold a men's tournament. In 2017, Eastbourne resumed hosting both men's and women's events.

American Taylor Fritz holds the record for the most men's titles at the tournament, with three wins. The champions from the last 10 editions are A. Roddick (USA/2012), F. Lopez (ESP/2013 and 2014), N. Djokovic (SRB/2017), A. Zverev (GER/2018), T. Fritz (USA/2019, 2022, and 2024), A. de Minaur (AUS/2021), and F. Cerundolo (ARG/2023).

Singles Winner:

Weeks 27-28 | 30 JUN | **London**
GRAND SLAM | The Championships, Wimbledon

The Wimbledon Championships, often simply called Wimbledon, are the oldest and most prestigious tennis tournament in the world. Since 1877, it has been held at the All England Lawn Tennis and Croquet Club in Wimbledon, London, and is played on grass courts. As of 2019, both the Centre Court and Court No. 1 are equipped with retractable roofs to reduce rain delays.

Wimbledon is one of the four Grand Slam tournaments, alongside the Australian Open, French Open, and US Open, and is the only one still played on grass, tennis' original surface. It is known for its strict traditions, such as a mandatory all-white dress code for players and royal patronage. Strawberries and cream, along with champagne, are iconic parts of the Wimbledon experience. The tournament maintains a minimal advertising presence, with Slazenger and Rolex among its long-standing official suppliers.

The first tournament took place in 1877, with only the gentlemen's singles competition. Spencer Gore won the inaugural final in front of about 200 spectators. Over time, Wimbledon has evolved, particularly after the introduction of the Open Era in 1968, allowing professional players to compete. The tournament has seen legendary players and matches, including British greats like Fred Perry and Andy Murray.

Wimbledon is considered the premier tennis event worldwide, with the club investing in long-term plans to enhance the experience for spectators and players alike. Recent developments include new courts, expanded facilities, and the addition of retractable roofs over Centre Court and Court No. 1.

In 2022, Wimbledon made headlines by banning Russian and Belarusian players due to the war in Ukraine, leading the ATP and WTA to withhold ranking points for that year's tournament. This decision was reversed in 2023, restoring normal ranking point allocation.

Wimbledon continues to stand as a symbol of tradition and excellence in tennis. The All England Club plans to acquire the adjacent Wimbledon Park Golf Club to host qualification matches on-site and further expand the complex, aiming to reinforce its position as the world's leading tennis tournament and maintain its high standards for players and spectators.

Wimbledon is renowned for unforgettable matches, including the longest match in tennis history, played between John Isner and Nicolas Mahut in 2010. Their first-round match lasted a total of 11 hours and 5 minutes, spanning three days. Isner finally won 70-68 in the fifth set. This epic match prompted the introduction of a tiebreak at 12-12 in the deciding set starting in 2021.

In 2001, Goran Ivanišević of Croatia made history by becoming the first wildcard player to win a Grand Slam when he triumphed at Wimbledon, defeating Patrick Rafter in a thrilling five-set final. Ivanišević had lost in three previous Wimbledon finals before achieving this remarkable victory.

Fred Perry was the last British man to win Wimbledon in 1936, a title drought that lasted 77 years until Andy Murray ended it in 2013 by defeating Novak Djokovic in the final. Murray's victory was a historic moment for British tennis.

Swiss legend Roger Federer holds the record for most Wimbledon titles with eight championships. The list of winners over the past decade includes N. Djokovic (SRB/2014, 2015, 2018, 2019, 2021, and 2022), A. Murray (GBR/2016), R. Federer (SUI/2017), and C. Alcaraz (ESP/2023 and 2024).

Singles Winner:

Week 29 | 14 JUL | **Bastad**
ATP 250 | Nordea Open

The Nordea Open, commonly known as the Swedish Open, is the only ATP tennis tournament in Scandinavia. The Swedish Open was first held in 1948 under the name International Swedish Hard Court Championships. The stadium, which seats 5,000 spectators, was renovated in 2002 to include a new hotel built into the stands by the sea. Magnus Gustafsson holds the record for the most tournament wins (4). The winners over the last 10 years include C. Berlocq (ARG/2013), P. Cuevas (URU/2014), B. Paire (FRA/2015), A. Ramos Vinolas (ESP/2016), D. Ferrer (ESP/2017), F. Fognini (ITA/2018), N. Jarry (CHI/2019), C. Ruud (NOR/2021), F. Cerundolo (ARG/2022), A. Rublev (RUS/2023), and N. Borges (POR/2024).

Singles Winner:

Week 29 | 14 JUL | **Gstaad**
ATP 250 | EFG Swiss Open Gstaad

The Swiss International Championships were founded in 1897 and originally held at the Grasshopper Club in Zurich. Over the years, the tournament has been hosted in various locations, including Gstaad. The first edition in Gstaad took place in 1915. Situated at 1,050 meters (3,450 feet) above sea level, Gstaad is the highest venue for ATP Tour events. Spaniards Alex Corretja and Sergi Bruguera share the record for most tournament wins at this location, with three titles each. The winners of the last 10 editions include M. Youzhny (RUS/2013), P. Andujar (ESP/2014), D. Thiem (AUT/2015), F. Lopez (ESP/2016), F. Fognini (ITA/2017), M. Berrettini (ITA/2018, 2024), A. Ramos Vinolas (ESP/2019), C. Ruud (NOR/2021, 2022), and P. Cachin (ARG/2023).

Singles Winner:

Week 29 | 14 JUL | **Los Cabos**
ATP 250 | Mifel Tennis Open by Telcel Oppo

Officially known as the Abierto de Tenis Mifel, this tournament takes place annually in the Baja California Sur region and is held on the outdoor courts of the Cabo del Mar Golf & Resort. Despite its smaller size, the Los Cabos Open consistently attracts top players looking to earn ranking points and prepare for the upcoming US Open. First held in 2016, the event also aims to promote tennis in Mexico. The picturesque setting and resort atmosphere make it a unique event.

Past winners include I. Karlovic (CRO/2016), S. Querrey (USA/2017), F. Fognini (ITA/2018), D. Schwartzman (ARG/2019), C. Norrie (GBR/2021), D. Medvedev (RUS/2022), S. Tsitsipas (GRE/2023), and J. Thompson (AUS/2024).

Singles Winner:

Week 30 | 20 JUL | **Kitzbuhel**
ATP 250 | Generali Open

The Austrian Open Kitzbühel is an annual tennis tournament held in Kitzbühel, Austria. Originally known as the Austrian International Championships from 1894 to 1968, it is one of the oldest and most prestigious events in the sport of tennis. Since 1894, the tournament has been played on clay courts at an altitude of 762 meters (2,500 feet) above sea level. Over the years, it has gone through various classifications, from the ATP World Series to the International Series Gold, and since 2009, it has been part of the ATP World Tour 250 series (except for 2010). The winners of the last 10 tournaments are: P. Kohlschreiber (GER/2015 and 2017), P. Lorenzi (ITA/2016), M. Klizan (SVK/2018), D. Thiem (AUT/2019), M. Kezmanovic (SRB/2020), C. Ruud (NOR/2021), R. Bautista Agut (ESP/2022), S. Baez (ARG/2023), and M. Berrettini (ITA/2024).

Singles Winner:

Week 30 | 20 JUL | **Umag**
ATP 250 | Plava Laguna Croatia Open Umag

The ATP tournament in Umag, officially known as the Plava Laguna Croatia Open Umag, is an annual tennis event held on clay courts in Umag, Croatia, since 1990. It falls under the ATP Tour 250 category and originally began as the Yugoslav Open. The venue is the ATP Stadium Goran Ivanišević, named after Croatia's most successful tennis player. The record holder for most tournament wins is Spaniard Carlos Moyá, who claimed the title five times. The winners of the last 10 tournaments are: P. Cuevas (URU/2014), D. Thiem (AUT/2015), F. Fognini (ITA/2016), A. Rublev (RUS/2017), M. Cecchinato (ITA/2018), D. Lajovic (CRO/2019), C. Alcaraz (ESP/2021), J. Sinner (ITA/2022), A. Popyrin (AUS/2023), and F. Cerundolo (ARG/2024).

Singles Winner:

Week 30 | 21 JUL | **Washington D.C.**
ATP 500| Mubadala DC Citi Open

The Washington Open is an annual tennis tournament played on hard courts at the William H.G. FitzGerald Tennis Center in Rock Creek Park, Washington, D.C. (Center Court seats 7,500 spectators). It is part of the ATP 500 series on the ATP Tour and the WTA 500 series on the WTA Tour. The tournament was first held in 1969 under the name Washington Star International and was played on clay courts until 1986, when it switched to hard courts. American Andre Agassi holds the local record with a total of five titles.

The winners of the last 10 tournaments are: M. Raonic (CAN/2014), K. Nishikori (JPN/2015), G. Monfils (FRA/2016), A. Zverev (GER/2017 and 2018), N. Kyrgios (AUS/2019 and 2022), J. Sinner (ITA/2021), D. Evans (USA/2023), and S. Korda (USA/2024).

Singles Winner:

Weeks 31-32 | 26 JUL | **Toronto**
ATP MASTERS 1000 | National Bank Open

The Canada Masters is officially known as the National Bank Open presented by Rogers. It is the sixth of nine tournaments in this category and is played on hard courts. Until 2019, the tournament alternated annually between Montreal (in odd-numbered years) and Toronto (in even-numbered years). Since 2021, it has been held in Montreal in even-numbered years and in Toronto in odd-numbered years.

The men's tournament has a long tradition dating back to 1881, making it one of the oldest tennis tournaments in the world, after Wimbledon. The women's competition was introduced in 1891, and a doubles competition has been held since 1924. In 1970, the Canadian Open became one of the founding members of the Grand Prix Tennis Circuit, and in 1990, the tournament was elevated to the highest category of the ATP Tour, the ATP Tour Masters 1000. Since 1997, the Canada and Cincinnati Masters have been held in back-to-back weeks, making it a notable achievement to win both tournaments in the same year – something only a few players have accomplished, including Rafael Nadal in 2013.

In Toronto, the tournament was held at the National Tennis Centre from 1976 to 2003, which seated 10,000 spectators. In 2004, Sobeys Stadium was opened on the same site, with a capacity of 12,500. In Montreal, the tournament is held at Stade IGA, which was opened in 1995 and seats 11,815. The tournament's record holder is Ivan Lendl, who triumphed six times in the 1980s.

The winners of the last 10 editions include: J-W. Tsonga (FRA/2014), A. Murray (GBR/2015), N. Djokovic (SRB/2016), A. Zverev (GER/2017), R. Nadal (ESP/2018 and 2019), D. Medvedev (RUS/2021), P. Carreno Busta (ESP/2022), J. Sinner (ITA/2023), and A. Popyrin (AUS/2024).

Singles Winner:

Weeks 32-33 | 7 AUG | **Cincinnati**
ATP MASTERS 1000 | Cincinnati Open

The Cincinnati Masters (officially known as the Cincinnati Open) is held on hard courts in Mason, Ohio, near Cincinnati. Like the Masters in Toronto held just before it, this tournament serves as a warm-up for the US Open.

The Cincinnati Masters has a long history and is one of the oldest tennis tournaments in the world. It was first held in 1899 at the Avondale Athletic Club, and since then, it has gone through various venues and surface types. Since 1979, the tournament has taken place at the Lindner Family Tennis Center in Mason. The main court has a seating capacity of 11,435. In the 1970s, the tournament was nearly removed from the tennis calendar, but today it is one of the largest tennis tournaments globally and has been a staple of the tennis season since the Masters Series was introduced. Between 1981 and 1989, it was part of the Grand Prix Super Series, the predecessor to the Masters.

Since 1997, the Cincinnati Masters and the Canada Masters have been held in consecutive weeks, similar to the spring tournaments in Indian Wells and Miami. It is considered a notable achievement to win both tournaments in the same year, something that has been accomplished by only a few players, including Patrick Rafter, Andy Roddick, and Rafael Nadal.

Swiss player Roger Federer holds the record for most Cincinnati Masters titles, having won it seven times. The winners of the last 10 editions are: R. Federer (SUI/2014 and 2015), M. Cilic (CRO/2016), G. Dimitrov (BUL/2017), N. Djokovic (SRB/2018, 2020, and 2023), D. Medvedev (RUS/2019), A. Zverev (GER/2021), B. Coric (CRO/2022), and F. Tiafoe (USA/2024).

Singles Winner:

Week 34 | 17 AUG | **Winston-Salem**
ATP 250 | Winston-Salem Open

The Winston-Salem Open is held at Wake Forest University in North Carolina. The tournament debuted in Winston-Salem in 2011 and is part of the ATP 250 category. Previously, it was held on Long Island and in New Haven before being sold and relocated to Winston-Salem. The event began in 1981 on Long Island as the Hamlet Challenge Cup, a small invitation tournament with four players that quickly developed into a larger competition. In the 1980s, players like Ivan Lendl and an 18-year-old Andre Agassi were among the winners. In 2005, the USTA decided to purchase the men's tournament from Long Island and combine it with the women's event in New Haven, creating the first major combined ATP-WTA event before the US Open. This combination lasted until 2011 when the men's competition was moved to Winston-Salem while the women stayed in New Haven.

The record holder for most titles in Winston-Salem is American John Isner, with two tournament victories. Other players who have won over the last 10 years include: J. Melzer (AUT/2013), L. Rosol (CZE/2014), K. Anderson (RSA/2015), P. Carreno Busta (ESP/2016), R. Bautista Agut (ESP/2017), D. Medvedev (RUS/2018), H. Hurkacz (POL/2019), I. Ivashka (BLR/2021), A. Mannarino (FRA/2022), S. Baez (ARG/2023), and L. Sonego (ITA/2024).

Singles Winner:

Weeks 35-36 | 25 AUG | **New York**
GRAND SLAM | US Open

The US Open Tennis Championships are a prestigious tennis tournament held annually on hard courts in Queens, New York. Since 1987, it has been the final event of the four Grand Slam tournaments in the tennis calendar, traditionally beginning on the last Monday in August and running for two weeks. The tournament's history dates back to 1881 when it was first played under the name U.S. National Championships. In its early years, only men competed in singles and doubles events.

Originally played on grass courts, the US Open transitioned to clay in 1975 to make the game more appealing for television. Since 1978, the tournament has been held on hard courts at the USTA Billie Jean King National Tennis Center in Flushing Meadows. The event boasts the largest stadium in the ATP Tour, the Arthur Ashe Stadium, which seats 23,771 spectators, along with the Louis Armstrong Stadium, which seats 14,053. The change in surfaces made Jimmy Connors the only player in the history of the tournament to win the title on all three: grass, clay, and hard courts.

The tournament is not only significant for its rich history but also for its pioneering innovations. In 1970, the US Open was the first Grand Slam to introduce tiebreakers to decide sets tied at 6-6, a rule that was later adopted by all the Grand Slam tournaments. Since 2022, all four Grand Slam events have adopted uniform tiebreak rules, with an extended tiebreak to 10 points in the deciding set.

The US Open is the only Grand Slam tournament that has been held every year without interruption since its inception. It was also the first major tournament to introduce the Hawk-Eye system in 2006 for reviewing line calls, enhancing the fairness and transparency of the game.

Since 2021, all line calls at the US Open have been made fully electronically through Hawk-Eye Live, once again placing the tournament at the forefront of technological advancements in tennis. The tournament is organized by the United States Tennis Association (USTA), a nonprofit organization that uses revenues from the event to promote the sport of tennis across the United States.

The US Open, with its long history and significance, holds many interesting aspects. For instance, American Andy Roddick was known for his powerful serves, and during the 2004 US Open, he set a personal speed record. His serve, clocked at around 244 km/h (152 mph), held the record for seven years until 2011. Moreover, John McEnroe, famous for his fiery temperament, delivered one of the most iconic outbursts in tennis history during the 1981 US Open. In a match against fellow American Tom Gullikson, McEnroe disagreed with a line call and shouted at the umpire, "You cannot be serious!"—a phrase that became synonymous with McEnroe's legacy.

Some of the all-time greats, including Pete Sampras, Jimmy Connors, and Roger Federer, each won the US Open five times in the Open Era.

The list of winners over the last 10 years includes: M. Cilic (CRO/2014), N. Djokovic (SRB/2015, 2018, and 2023), S. Wawrinka (SUI/2016), R. Nadal (ESP/2017 and 2019), D. Thiem (AUT/2020), D. Medvedev (RUS/2021), C. Alcaraz (ESP/2022), and J. Sinner (ITA/2024).

Singles Winner:

Week 38 | 17 SEP | **Chengdu**
ATP 250 | Chengdu Open

The Chengdu Open is held on outdoor hard courts at the Sichuan International Tennis Center. It replaced the tournament in Kuala Lumpur (Malaysia) in 2016 and is classified as an ATP Tour 250 event. The tournament features a 28-player singles draw and a 16-team doubles draw, making it the highest-paying tournament in its category. It takes place annually in September, running concurrently with the tournament in Zhuhai. After a three-year hiatus due to the COVID-19 pandemic, the tournament resumed in 2023.

Due to the tournament's relatively young history, the list of winners is still quite short: K. Khachanov (RUS/2016), D. Istomin (UZB/2017), B. Tomic (AUS/2018), P. Carreno Busta (ESP/2019), and A. Zverev (GER/2023).

Singles Winner:

Week 38 | 17 SEP | **Zhuhai**
ATP 250| Huafa Properties Zhuhai Championsh.

The Zhuhai Championships, officially known as the Huajin Securities Zhuhai Championships, is held on outdoor hard courts. It was first held in 2014 and replaced the tournament in Bangkok. Initially, the tournament took place for five years at the Shenzhen Longgang Sports Center in Shenzhen before moving to the Hengqin International Tennis Center in Zhuhai in 2019 (Center Court: 3,983 seats). The tournament runs concurrently with the event held in Chengdu, China. The event was not held from 2020 to 2022 due to COVID-19.

The list of winners is still very short and includes: A. de Minaur (AUS/2019) and K. Khachanov (RUS/2023).

Singles Winner:

Week 39 | 24 SEP | **Beijing**
ATP 500 | China Open

Originally founded in 1993 as the Beijing Open, it was first held at the Tsinghua University Sports Hall. Nowadays, the tournament takes place on outdoor hard courts at the National Tennis Center and is held from late September to early October. Since 2004, the tournament has been held in its current form, with the first combined event for men and women taking place in 2008. Serbian player Novak Djokovic is the only player to have won the men's singles title six times, remaining undefeated. The list of winners from the last 10 events includes: T. Berdych (CZE/2011), N. Djokovic (SRB/2012-2015), A. Murray (GBR/2016), R. Nadal (ESP/2017), N. Basilashvili (GEO/2018), D. Thiem (AUT/2019), and J. Sinner (ITA/2023).

Singles Winner:

Week 39 | 24 SEP | **Tokyo**
ATP 500| Kinoshita Group Japan Open Tennis Ch.

The Japan Open is held at the Ariake Tennis Forest Park in Koto, Tokyo, with the Ariake Coliseum (10,000 seats) as the main court. The tournament has its origins in the All-Japan Championships, which were founded in 1915 and later known as the Japan International Championships. The local record holder is Swedish player Stefan Edberg, who has won the tournament a total of four times. The winners list from the last 10 events features nine different players: K. Nishikori (JPN/2012 and 2014), J. M. del Potro (ARG/2013), S. Wawrinka (SUI/2015), N. Kyrgios (AUS/2016), D. Goffin (BEL/2017), D. Medvedev (RUS/2018), N. Djokovic (SRB/2019), T. Fritz (USA/2022), and B. Shelton (USA/2023).

Singles Winner:

Weeks 40-41 | 1 OCT | **Shanghai**
ATP MASTERS 1000 | Rolex Shanghai Masters

The Shanghai Rolex Masters is played on outdoor hard courts at the Qizhong Forest Sports City Arena in the Minhang District. The tournament is part of the ATP Tour Masters 1000 category and is the only one of these events not held in Europe or North America. In the early 2000s, Shanghai hosted the Tennis Masters Cup, which eventually led to the establishment of the Shanghai Masters as an ATP Masters 1000 tournament.

The Qizhong Arena, originally built in 2004 and 2005 to host the Tennis Masters Cup, is the largest tennis stadium in Asia, featuring a main stadium with 15,000 seats and a retractable roof. The tournament was inaugurated in 2009 after the ATP and the Chinese Tennis Association sought to further develop the tennis market in China and Asia.

From 2020 to 2022, the tournament was not held due to travel restrictions related to the COVID-19 pandemic. In 2023, a total prize money of $8.8 million was awarded. The local record holder for most tournament wins is Serbia's Novak Djokovic, with a total of 4 titles. Additionally, the winners list from the last 10 tournaments includes the following players: A. Murray (GBR/2011 and 2016), N. Djokovic (SRB/2012, 2013, 2015, and 2018), R. Federer (SUI/2014 and 2017), D. Medvedev (RUS/2019), and H. Hurkacz (POL/2023).

Singles Winner:

Week 42 | 13 OCT | **Almaty**
ATP 250 | Almaty Open

The Almaty Open (formerly the Astana Open) is a professional tennis tournament held on indoor hard courts in Kazakhstan. The tournament was originally established due to the cancellation of many events during the 2020 season as a result of the COVID-19 pandemic.

The event was held as an ATP 250 tournament in 2020, 2021, and 2023, and as an ATP 500 event in 2022. In 2024, the tournament was relocated from its original venue in Astana (the capital of Kazakhstan) to Almaty.

The winners list includes J. Millman (AUS/2020), K. Soon-woo (KOR/2021), N. Djokovic (SRB/2022), and A. Mannarino (FRA/2023).

Singles Winner:

Week 42 | 13 OCT | **Antwerp**
ATP 250 | European Open

The tournament was initially held in Antwerp from 1982 to 1998. After a long hiatus, it has been held annually again since 2016, as the successor to the Valencia Open. Originally, the event was an invitational tournament until 1992, with no world ranking points awarded. A unique highlight was the "Gold Racquet"—a life-sized tennis racquet made of gold, adorned with 1,420 diamonds (valued at 1 million USD), awarded to a player who won the tournament three times within five years. Ivan Lendl was the only player to achieve this feat.

The winners list since 2016 includes: R. Gasquet (FRA/2016), J.-W. Tsonga (FRA/2017), K. Edmund (GBR/2018), A. Murray (GBR/2019), U. Humbert (FRA/2020), J. Sinner (ITA/2021), F. Auger-Aliassime (CAN/2022), and A. Bublik (KAZ/2023).

Singles Winner:

Week 42 | 13 OCT | **Stockholm**
ATP 250 | BNP Parisbas Nordic Open

The tournament was founded in 1969 and is still mostly held at the Kungliga Tennishallen, with the exception of the years 1989 to 1994 when it took place in the Ericsson Globe Arena. Since 1995, the tournament has been classified as an ATP Tour 250 event. Notable tournament directors include former Swedish professional players Robin Söderling (2014 and 2015) and, since 2016, Simon Aspelin. The local record holders are John McEnroe and Boris Becker, each with four titles.

Additionally, the winners list includes G. Dimitrov (BUL/2013), T. Berdych (CZE/2014 and 2015), J.-M. del Potro (ARG/2016 and 2017), S. Tsitsipas (GRE/2018), D. Shapovalov (CAN/2019), T. Paul (USA/2021), H. Rune (DEN/2022), and G. Monfils (FRA/2023).

Singles Winner:

Week 43 | 20 OCT | **Basel**
ATP 500 | Swiss Indoors Basel

The tournament is held on indoor hard courts at the St. Jakobshalle in Münchenstein, near Basel. It was founded by Roger Brennwald and initially took place on a small scale without doubles matches in an inflatable hall. Since 1975, it has been held at the St. Jakobshalle. Over the years, the surface has alternated between carpet and hard court, but since 2007 it has been consistently played on hard courts. In 2009, the tournament was upgraded to ATP Tour 500 status. Swiss player Roger Federer has won the tournament ten times (with 15 finals appearances).

The winners list from the past 10 tournaments includes J.-M. del Potro (ARG/2012 and 2013), R. Federer (SUI/2014, 2015, 2017-2019), M. Cilic (CRO/2016), and F. Auger-Aliassime (FRA/2022 and 2023).

Singles Winner:

Week 43 | 20 OCT | **Wien**
ATP 500 | Erste Bank Open

The tournament has been held annually in October at the Wiener Stadthalle in Rudolfsheim-Fünfhaus on the Rebound Ace hard court surface since 1974. It is one of two ATP Tour events in Austria and takes place simultaneously with the tournament in Basel. Initially played on carpet courts, the surface switched to various hard courts before Rebound Ace was introduced in 2015. Over the years, the tournament has attracted many young talents like Ivan Lendl, Roger Federer, and Novak Dokovic, as well as established stars like Pete Sampras, Boris Becker, and Andre Agassi.

Austrian players such as Thomas Muster, Jürgen Melzer, and Dominic Thiem have also participated regularly. After being downgraded to ATP Tour 250 status from 2009 to 2015, the tournament has been part of the ATP Tour 500 since 2015.

The local record holder for most tournament wins is American Brian Gottfried with four titles. Additionally, the winners of the last 10 tournaments include: A. Murray (GBR/2014 and 2016), D. Ferrer (ESP/2015), L. Pouille (FRA/2017), K. Anderson (RSA/2018), D. Thiem (AUT/2019), A. Rublev (RUS/2020), A. Zverev (GER/2021), D. Medvedev (RUS/2022), and J. Sinner (ITA/2023).

Singles Winner:

Week 44 | 27 OCT | **Paris**
ATP MASTERS 1000 | Rolex Paris Masters

The Paris Masters, formerly known as the Paris Open and currently called the Rolex Paris Masters for sponsorship reasons, is held at the AccorHotels Arena (seating capacity: 15,609) in the Bercy district of Paris. It is an indoor hard court tournament and the final Masters event of the season before the ATP Finals.

The tournament originally evolved from the French Covered Court Championships and, starting in the Open Era, was held at the Stade Pierre de Coubertin until 1982. In 1989, it became part of the Grand Prix Super Series. The tournament is often referred to as the "Paris Indoor" or simply "Bercy" to distinguish it from the other major Parisian tennis event, the French Open, which is played outdoors.

The Paris Masters was once known for its fast surface, which favored bold, aggressive play. However, since 2011, the court has been slowed down, aligning with the general trend on the tour. Ilie Năstase, Andre Agassi, Roger Federer, and Novak Djokovic are the only players to have won both the Paris Masters and the French Open. Năstase, Agassi, and Djokovic even managed to win both tournaments in the same season, with Djokovic achieving this feat twice.

The local record holder for the most titles is Serbia's Novak Djokovic, with 7 titles out of 9 final appearances. Additionally, the list of winners from the last 10 tournaments includes: N. Djokovic (SRB/2014, 2015, 2019, 2021, 2023), A. Murray (GBR/2016), J. Sock (USA/2017), K. Khachanov (RUS/2018), D. Medvedev (RUS/2020), and H. Rune (DEN/2022).

Singles Winner:

Week 45 | 2 NOV | **Metz**
ATP 250 | Moselle Open

The ATP tournament in Metz is played on indoor hard courts. It was first held in 2003 and moved between various venues in the following years. Since 2014, it has returned to being hosted in the Arènes de Metz. The Moselle Open is one of four French tournaments in the ATP Tour 250 category. The record singles champion is Jo-Wilfried Tsonga, with four titles. Arnaud Clément and Hubert Hurkacz are the only players to have won both singles and doubles in Metz.

The list of winners from the last 10 tournaments includes: G. Simon (FRA/2013, 2018), D. Goffin (BEL/2014), J.-W. Tsonga (FRA/2015, 2019), L. Pouille (FRA/2016), P. Gojowczyk (GER/2017), H. Hurkacz (POL/2021), L. Sonego (ITA/2022), and U. Humbert (FRA/2023).

Singles Winner:

Week 45 | 2 NOV | **Gijon**
ATP 250| Watergen Gijon Open

The ATP tournament in Gijón, officially known as the Watergen Gijón Open, is a men's tennis tournament on the ATP Tour that was first held in 2022 in the Spanish city of Gijón, played indoors on hard courts. It was introduced in response to the COVID-19 pandemic, as many tournaments in the 2022 ATP calendar were canceled or postponed. The tournament is part of the ATP Tour 250 category, featuring a singles draw of 28 players and 16 doubles teams, with the top four seeds receiving a first-round bye.

After a one-year hiatus, the tournament returned to the ATP calendar in 2024 and is scheduled to be held in November at the Palacio de Deportes de Gijón, supported by the Spanish Tennis Federation. The only winner so far (2022) was A. Rublev (RUS).

Singles Winner:

Week 46 | 9 NOV | **Turin**
ATP FINALS | Nitto ATP Finals

The ATP Finals are the season-ending tournament of the ATP Tour and, after the four Grand Slam tournaments, are considered the most prestigious event in men's tennis. First held in 1970, the tournament brings together the top eight singles players and the top eight doubles teams of the year based on their ATP Race standings, which reflect their results throughout the season. The eighth spot may be awarded to a player or team who has won a Grand Slam title that year and is ranked between ninth and twentieth in the world rankings.

A unique feature of the ATP Finals is the tournament format, which differs from other ATP events. Instead of a simple knockout system, the participants first compete in a round-robin group stage. The singles players and doubles teams are divided into two groups of four. Each group plays a round-robin format, meaning each participant plays three matches against the others in their group. The top two players or teams from each group advance to the semifinals, followed by a final to determine the champion. This format allows a player or team to progress even after losing a match in the group stage.

The history of the ATP Finals is marked by numerous changes and adaptations. Initially known as the "Masters Grand Prix" and part of the Grand Prix Tennis Circuit, the tournament was taken over by the ATP in 1990 and renamed the "ATP Tour World Championships." From then on, ranking points were awarded, increasing the tournament's significance. Between 2000 and 2008, the event was called the "Tennis Masters Cup," before being rebranded as the "ATP World Tour Finals" in 2009 and later simplified to "ATP Finals" in 2017. Over the years, the event has been hosted in various cities, including Tokyo, Paris, and New York, before settling in London from 2009 to 2020. Since 2021, the tournament has been held in Turin, Italy, with plans to remain there until 2025.

In recent years, the ATP Finals have established themselves as the most important indoor tournament in the world, a status underscored by the high prize money awarded. Serbian player Novak Djokovic holds the record for the most singles titles, with seven victories. In 2022, Djokovic also won the highest prize money ever awarded at a tennis tournament, amounting to $4,740,300. In addition to the substantial cash prizes, winners of the ATP Finals can earn up to 1,500 ranking points if they navigate the tournament undefeated.

The ATP Finals have evolved over the years and gained significance, attracting the best players in the world. The round-robin format, followed by knockout matches, creates an exciting and dynamic conclusion to the tennis season. The controlled conditions of an indoor tournament, such as playing on hard courts and the precise lighting, contribute to the unique atmosphere of this prestigious event. Currently, the tournament is held at the Palasport Olimpico in Turin.

The list of winners from the last ten events includes the following players: N. Djokovic (SRB/2014, 2015, 2022, and 2023), A. Murray (GBR/2016), G. Dimitrov (BUL/2017), A. Zverev (GER/2018 and 2021), S. Tsitsipas (GRE/2019), and D. Medvedev (RUS/2020).

Singles Winner:

LIST OF TOURNAMENT WINNERS

Tournament	Name of Player
ATP 250 | Brisbane	_____
ATP 250 | Hong Kong	_____
ATP 250 | Adelaide	_____
ATP 250 | Auckland	_____
GS | Australian Open	_____
ATP 250 | Montpellier	_____
ATP 500 | Dallas	_____
ATP 500 | Rotterdam	_____
ATP 250 | Buenos Aires	_____
ATP 250 | Delray Beach	_____
ATP 250 | Marseille	_____
ATP 500 | Doha	_____
ATP 500 | Rio de Janeiro	_____
ATP 500 | Acapulco	_____
ATP 500 | Dubai	_____
ATP 250 | Santiago de C.	_____
MASTERS | Indian Wells	_____
MASTERS | Miami	_____
ATP 250 | Bukarest	_____
ATP 250 | Houston	_____
ATP 250 | Marrakech	_____
MASTERS | Monte Carlo	_____

LIST OF TOURNAMENT WINNERS

Tournament	Name of Player
ATP 500 | **Barcelona**	_____
ATP 500 | **München**	_____
MASTERS | **Madrid**	_____
MASTERS | **Rom**	_____
ATP 500 | **Hamburg**	_____
ATP 250 | **Genf**	_____
GS | **French Open**	_____
ATP 250 | **'S-Hertogenbosch**	_____
ATP 250 | **Stuttgart**	_____
ATP 500 | **Halle**	_____
ATP 500 | **London**	_____
ATP 250 | **Mallorca**	_____
ATP 250 | **Eastburne**	_____
GS | **Wimbledon**	_____
ATP 250 | **Bastad**	_____
ATP 250 | **Gstaad**	_____
ATP 250 | **Los Cabos**	_____
ATP 250 | **Kitzbühel**	_____
ATP 250 | **Umag**	_____
ATP 500 | **Washington**	_____
MASTERS | **Toronto**	_____
MASTERS | **Cincinnati**	_____

LIST OF TOURNAMENT WINNERS

Tournament	Name of Player
ATP 250	Winston-Salem	
GS	US Open	
ATP 250	Chengdu	
ATP 250	Zhuhai	
ATP 500	Tokio	
ATP 500	Peking	
MASTERS	Shanghai	
ATP 250	Almaty	
ATP 250	Antwerpen	
ATP 250	Stockholm	
ATP 500	Basel	
ATP 500	Wien	
MASTERS	Paris	
ATP 250	Metz	
ATP 250	Gijon	
ATP Finals	Nitto ATP Finals	

TOP 20 - AT THE END OF THE SEASON 2025

	Name of Player	Points

No. 1: _____

No. 2: _____

No. 3: _____

No. 4: _____

No. 5: _____

No. 6: _____

No. 7: _____

No. 8: _____

No. 9: _____

No. 10: _____

No. 11: _____

No. 12: _____

No. 13: _____

No. 14: _____

No. 15: _____

No. 16: _____

No. 17: _____

No. 18: _____

No. 19: _____

No. 20: _____

QUIZ

Congratulations on making it this far! You've learned a lot about the exciting world of the ATP men's tour, its glamorous tournaments, fascinating history, and unforgettable highlights. Now it's time to put your knowledge to the test!

Are you ready to showcase your tennis skills and find out just how well you know ATP men's tennis? Grab your virtual racket, and let's get started! Whether you're just beginning your journey or you're an absolute tennis pro, this quiz has something for everyone.

Test your knowledge with our 30 exciting questions and see if you can become a "Grand Slam Champion" or if you still need a bit more practice. At the end, you'll not only find the correct answers but also a fun categorization of winners to show you where you stand in the tennis universe.

So, have fun playing and good luck! Who knows, you might just become the next tennis expert!

Questions

1. Who holds the record for the most ATP singles titles?
   a) Roger Federer
   b) Jimmy Connors
   c) Rafael Nadal
2. In which years was the ATP founded?
   a) 1990
   b) 1988
   c) 1995
3. Which player has won the most Grand Slam titles in men's singles?
   a) Novak Djokovic
   b) Roger Federer
   c) Rafael Nadal
4. Which one does not belong to the ATP Masters 1000 series?
   a) Wimbledon
   b) Monte Carlo Masters
   c) Indian Wells Masters
5. Who was the youngest player to ever win the ATP Finals?
   a) Boris Becker
   b) Pete Sampras
   c) Andre Agassi
6. How many Grand Slam tournaments are there in men's tennis?
   a) 3
   b) 4
   c) 5
7. What surface is used at the French Open?
   a) Hard court
   b) Grass
   c) Clay
8. Who won the ATP Finals in 2021?
   a) Alexander Zverev
   b) Daniil Medvedev
   c) Novak Djokovic

9. Which player was the first to win all four Grand Slam tournaments at least twice?
   a) Roger Federer
   b) Novak Djokovic
   c) Rod Laver
10. On what surface is the Wimbledon tournament played?
   a) Grass
   b) Hard court
   c) Clay
11. Which player has won the most ATP Masters 1000 titles?
   a) Rafael Nadal
   b) Roger Federer
   c) Novak Djokovic
12. How many sets must a player win in men's singles to win a match at Grand Slam tournaments?
   a) 2
   b) 3
   c) 4
13. Who won the longest tennis match in history, which lasted 11 hours and 5 minutes?
   a) John Isner
   b) Nicolas Mahut
   c) Andy Roddick
14. How many players compete in the singles event at the ATP Finals?
   a) 6
   b) 8
   c) 10
15. Who was the oldest player to ever win the ATP Finals?
   a) Andre Agassi
   b) Roger Federer
   c) Novak Djokovic

16. Which city hosted the ATP Finals from 2009 to 2020?
    a) Madrid
    b) London
    c) New York
17. Which player has the most wins on clay in men's tennis?
    a) Roger Federer
    b) Rafael Nadal
    c) Novak Djokovic
18. How many times has Roger Federer won Wimbledon?
    a) 6
    b) 7
    c) 8
19. Who won the ATP Finals in 2022?
    a) Novak Djokovic
    b) Daniil Medvedev
    c) Carlos Alcaraz
20. Who is the youngest player to ever win an ATP Tour singles tournament?
    a) Rafael Nadal
    b) Lleyton Hewitt
    c) Michael Chang
21. Which player has won the "Golden Slam" in men's singles (all four Grand Slams and an Olympic gold medal in the same year)?
    a) Rod Laver
    b) Rafael Nadal
    c) No Player
22. What color is the surface at the ATP Masters in Madrid?
    a) Blue
    b) Red
    c) Green
23. Which player holds the record for the most weeks as the number 1 in the ATP rankings?
    a) Pete Sampras
    b) Novak Djokovic
    c) Roger Federer

24. What is the term for winning all four Grand Slam tournaments within a calendar year?
    a) Carreer Grand Slam
    b) Golden Slam
    c) Calender Grand Slam

25. Which player was the first in ATP Tour history to win 20 Grand Slam titles?
    a) Rafael Nadal
    b) Novak Djokovic
    c) Roger Federer

26. What is the most common surface on the ATP Tour?
    a) Hard Court
    b) Clay
    c) Grass

27. Which player is known as the „King of Clay"?
    a) Novak Djokovic
    b) Rafael Nadal
    c) Roger Federer

28. Which Australian first won the ATP Tour World Championship?
    a) Patrick Rafter
    b) Lleyton Hewitt
    c) Mark Philippoussis

29. Who served the most aces in a single match?
    a) Ivo Karlović
    b) John Isner
    c) Goran Ivanišević

30. How many Grand Slam titles has Andy Murray won?
    a) 2
    b) 3
    c) 4

Answers

1. b) Jimmy Connors
2. a) 1990
3. c) Rafael Nadal
4. a) Wimbledon
5. a) Boris Becker
6. b) 4
7. c) Clay
8. a) Alexander Zverev
9. b) Novak Djokovic
10. a) Grass
11. c) Novak Djokovic
12. b) 3
13. a) John Isner
14. b) 8
15. c) Novak Djokovic
16. b) London
17. b) Rafael Nadal
18. c) 8
19. a) Novak Djokovic
20. c) Michael Chang
21. c) no player
22. a) Blue
23. b) Novak Djokovic
24. c) Calender Grand Slam
25. c) Roger Federer
26. a) Hard Court
27. b) Rafael Nadal
28. b) Lleyton Hewitt
29. b) John Isner
30. b) 3

Winner Categories

0-7 Points: "Ball Boy or Ball Girl"
You're still at the beginning of your tennis journey, learning the basic rules and key facts of the ATP Tour. As a "ball boy or ball girl," you collect the balls and closely observe the action on the court. You're eager to learn more about the world of tennis. With a bit more practice and time, you'll surely improve!

8-15 Points: "Service Ace"
You already have a solid foundational knowledge of the ATP Tour and its stars. Like a serve ace on the court that dominates the first rally, you've developed a good sense for the essential aspects of the game. You know the key tournaments and players and have some interesting facts up your sleeve. With a little more effort and training, you'll surely be among the top players soon!

16-23 Points: "Baseline-Expert"
You are already a true pro when it comes to tennis knowledge. As a "Baseline Expert," you master the basic and advanced shots on the court and are always ready to challenge your opponent. You have a good understanding of the history and intricacies of the ATP Tour and know what it takes to be a successful player. Keep it up— with this knowledge, you will win many matches to come!

24-30 Points: "Grand Slam Champion"
Congratulations! You have excelled in the quiz and are a true tennis connoisseur! As a "Grand Slam Champion," you demonstrate your comprehensive knowledge of the ATP Tour, its players, tournaments, and historical moments. You not only know the big names and events but also the little details that make the sport of tennis so fascinating. With your knowledge, you could be a part of the ATP Tour or shine as a tennis expert. Fantastic job!

Copyright © 2024
Dieter Haselsteiner
Aichen 3
3240 Mank

All rights reserved
ISBN: 9798342967860
Self Publishing

Printed by Amazon Kindle Direct Publishing
Image sources: Canva.com

This work, including all its parts, is protected by copyright. Any use is prohibited without the author's consent. This applies in particular to reproductions, translations, microfilming, and the storage and processing in electronic systems.
The use of this book and the implementation of the information contained therein is expressly at your own risk. Claims for damages against the publisher and the author for material or immaterial damage caused by the use or non-use of the information or by the use of erroneous and/or incomplete information are fundamentally excluded. Legal claims for damages are therefore excluded. The work, including all contents, has been prepared with the utmost care. However, the publisher and the author do not guarantee the timeliness, correctness, completeness, and quality of the information provided. Printing errors and misinformation cannot be completely ruled out. The publisher and the author are also not liable for the timeliness, accuracy, and completeness of the contents of the book, nor for printing errors.
No legal responsibility or liability in any form for erroneous statements and the resulting consequences can be assumed by the publisher or the author. The operators of the respective websites referred to in this book are solely responsible for the content of those websites.

The publisher and the author have no influence on the design and content of external websites. Therefore, the publisher and the author distance themselves from all external content. At the time of use, there were no illegal contents on the websites.

Printed in Great Britain
by Amazon